Start TO Finish
Second Series

FROM Cub TO Tiger

JENNIFER BOOTHROYD

LERNER PUBLICATIONS Minneapolis

TABLE OF Contents

Lerner Publications Company
A division of Lerner Publishing Group, Inc.
241 First Avenue North
Minneapolis, MN 55401 USA

For reading levels and more information, look up this title at www.lernerbooks.com.

Library of Congress Cataloging-in-Publication Data

The Cataloging-in-Publication Data for *From Cub to Tiger*
   is on file at the Library of Congress.
ISBN 978-1-5124-1832-3 (lib. bdg.)
ISBN 978-1-5124-1835-4 (pbk.)
ISBN 978-1-5124-1836-1 (EB pdf)

Manufactured in the United States of America
1-41176-23184-3/23/2016

Tigers are big cats. How do they grow?

First, a tigress finds a safe home.

Shortly before a tigress is ready to give birth, she looks for a den. She'll need a place to hide her cubs while she goes out to hunt prey.

Then a litter of tiny cubs is born.

There are usually two to four cubs in a litter. Newborn cubs typically weigh between 2 and 3 pounds (0.9 and 1.4 kilograms). The cubs are born with their eyes closed. They depend on their mother for food and protection.

Next, their eyes open.

Newborn cubs spend most of their time sleeping and drinking milk from their mother. Within a few weeks, their eyes open and the cubs are able to see.

Then the cubs begin to eat solid food.

When they are about two months old, the cubs'
mother brings meat for them to eat. They use their
baby teeth to tear the meat. Their permanent
teeth will come in before they are one year old.

Soon the cubs can leave the den.

The cubs still stay close to their mother, but the family roams through more of their territory. The mother's paws leave a scent on the ground that the cubs can use to follow her.

The cubs continue to develop new skills.

The cubs play together by wrestling and pouncing.
They get stronger by practicing moves that will
help them hunt.

The cubs start learning to hunt.

When they are eight months old, the cubs no longer drink their mother's milk. They go on hunts with their mother and watch her closely. The cubs learn to slowly and silently **stalk** their prey.

Finally, the cubs can live on their own.

By the time they are two years old, the cubs are ready to leave their mother. Fully grown tigers can weigh between 165 and 570 pounds (75 to 259 kg).

Soon the tigers will have their own cubs.

Female tigers typically have a litter every two years. Only half of the cubs born in the wild survive to adulthood. Wild tigers can live for ten years or more.

Glossary

cubs: baby tigers

den: an animal's shelter

litter: babies born to an animal at one time

prey: an animal that is hunted for food by another animal

roams: walks around an area

stalk: to quietly follow something

territory: the area an animal claims for its own

tigress: a female tiger

Further Information

Franchino, Vicky. *Tigers*. New York: Children's Press, 2012. Explore some issues affecting tiger survival and how humans can help.

Hirsch, Rebecca E. *Siberian Tigers: Camouflaged Hunting Mammals*. Minneapolis: Lerner Publications, 2015. Learn how a tiger's traits help it survive in the wild.

Marsh, Laura. *Tigers*. Washington, DC: National Geographic, 2012. Discover fascinating facts about powerful tigers.

National Geographic Kids: 5 Reasons Why Tigers Are Terrific
http://kids.nationalgeographic.com/explore/5-reasons-why-hub/5-reasons-tigers-are-terrific
Learn a few key facts about tiger behavior.

San Diego Zoo Kids
http://kids.sandiegozoo.org/animals/mammals/tiger
Watch videos, view photos, and read facts about tigers living in the wild and at the zoo.

Index

Photo Acknowledgments
The images in this book are used with the permission of:
© Anankkml/Dreamstime.com, p. 1; © Sanjeev Kumar/
Dreamstime.com, p. 3; © Ss IMAGES/Alamy, p. 5;
© Barcroft Media/Getty Images, p. 7; © Suzi Eszterhas/
Minden Pictures, p. 9; © Keith Barlow/Dreamstime.com,
p. 11; © Aditya "Dicky" Singh/Alamy, p. 13; © Bildagentur
Zoonar GmbH/Shutterstock, p. 15; © Abhishek Singh/
Dreamstime.com, p. 17; © Theo Allofs/Minden Pictures,
p. 19; © Juniors/Juniors/SuperStock, p. 21.

Front cover: © iStockphoto.com/
MarkMalkinsonPhotography.

Main body text set in Arta Std Book 20/26.
Typeface provided by International Typeface Corp.

LERNER

SOURCE™

Expand learning beyond the printed book. Download free, complementary
educational resources for this book from our website, www.lerneresource.com.